CANELO ÁLVAREZ

A SHORT UNAUTHORIZED BIOGRAPHY

FAME LIFE BIOS

CHAPTER 1

WHO IS CANELO ÁLVAREZ?

SANTOS SAÚL ÁLVAREZ BARRAGÁN, more famous for his boxer moniker "Canelo," is a Mexican professional boxer. His nickname means cinnamon in English, a common nickname for red-haired people in Mexico. He holds four-division world titles. He was named the world's best active boxer in October 2020 by publications Boxing Writers Association of America, BoxRec, The Ring, the TBRB, and ranked second by ESPN. Since 2018, he has earned WBA (Super) titles, The Ring and lineal middleweight, and the WBA (Regular) super middleweight title. From 2011 to 2013, he originally owned the WBA (Unified), WBC, and Ring light middleweight titles; from 2015 to 2019, the WBC (twice), Ring and linear middleweight titles; from 2016 to 2017, the WBO light-middleweight title; and the IBF middleweight and WBO light heavyweight titles in 2019.

. . .

Álvarez was born on July 18, 1990, to parents Santos and Ana Maria Barragan. The boxer's humble beginnings in the sport started in the Álvarez family farm when he was inspired by his oldest brother Rigoberto. Rigo gave him his first pair of gloves when he was 10. The eldest brother turned pro when young Canelo was only 13 years old. He found his way to Julian Magdaleno Gymnasium, where Chepo and Eddy's father-son duo taught him.

His amateur record was 44-2, 12 of them knockouts. Chepo stated that Álvarez had bouts that weren't accounted for and lacked documentation, but it would be laborious to dig those up. To date, his professional record is 53-1 with two draws. His only loss was to Floyd Mayweather.Álvarez is renowned as an exceptional counterpuncher, capable of manipulating openings in his rivals' defenses while preventing head and body movement blows. He is also known as a spectacular body puncher. It is also labeled the world's best effective middleweight by BoxRec, The Ring, and TBRB, the world's fourth-best influential super middleweight by The Ring, the fifth by TBRB, and the world's third-best active lightweight by TBRB.

In 2019, Forbes rated Saul Alvarez, often portrayed in the mainstream as Canelo, one of the highest-paid players worldwide. For any celebrities internationally, that accomplishment is among the most prestigious. With over 15 years of experience in the sport, Canelo Álvarez is a decorated boxer. He holds The Ring magazine titles middleweight and light middleweight, the lineal title middleweight twice, regional titles Jalisco welterweight, WBA Fedecentro welterweight, WBC-NABF welterweight, WBO Latino welterweight, WBC Youth welterweight, WBC Silver light middleweight, and honorary titles WBC Diamond middle-weight title, WBC Franchise middleweight title.

CHAPTER 2

THINGS PEOPLE HAVE SAID ABOUT CANELO ÁLVAREZ

WITH FOUR-DIVISION WORLD championships on his belt, Canelo Álvarez is definitely on top of his career. "He hasn't finished his career, but on the day he retires, I have full confidence he will be considered the best in all aspects —titles, money, achievements," Alvarez's trainer Eddy Reynoso shared.

The boxing star's past opponents say he is a strong contender. British professional boxer Liam Smith revealed that he watched Álvarez as a fan before it was realized that their bout could happen. His variety in the attack was his biggest strength. Austin Trout, who Álvarez defeated in 2013, explained that he is not only a good fighter but a smart one at that. Furthermore, his speed and power are factors that make him "exciting for the sport."

CHAPTER 3

CANELO ÁLVAREZ IS BORN

SANTOS SAÚL ÁLVAREZ BARRAGÁN, or commonly known as Canelo Álvarez, was born in Guadalajara, Jalisco, Mexico, on July 18, 1990. He was born the youngest of eight children, seven boys and one girl, to Ana Maria Barragan and Santos Álvarez. The family lived in his birth city until he was five years old, then moved to Juanacatlán, Jalisco.

Both of Álvarez's parents, Ana Maria and Santos, are farmers. Also, his father owned an ice cream parlor with three branches when he was young. Álvarez grew up poor on the farm where they lived and always had a job. When he was 15 years old, his parents separated.

Canelo is a father and a husband. He's in close touch with his four children, his multiple siblings, and, of course, his parents. His father's name is Santos Alvarez. Santos had seven boys (including Canelo) and one girl with his long-time wife, Ana María Barragán. The player's parents got divorced in 2005. In 2005, Santos Álvarez got involved with another woman soon after the divorce. A year later, they welcomed a baby boy named Bryan. The two separated shortly after the baby's birth.

By nationality, Álvarez is Mexican, and his ethnic group is white. His mother's surname Barragán is said to be Spanish in origin. It is believed that he has Irish ancestry, though a connection was not established. Álvarez went on record to say that "there might have been an Irish grandfather somewhere there in my past." His famously red hair was inherited from his mother, Ana Maria. His sister also shares the same hair color.

CHAPTER 4

GROWING UP WITH CANELO ÁLVAREZ

THE MIDDLE-CLASS FAMILY lived on a farm where they raised all their children Rigoberto, Gonzalo, Daniel, Ramon, Ricardo, Victor, Daniel, Ana, and Canelo. Like him, all his brothers used to work on the farm and their ice cream business before venturing to do boxing. All seven of the Álvarez boys forayed into the boxing world while Ana, the only girl, managed a business. Although his parents divorced, both Ana Maria and Santos stayed supportive of him throughout the years. Álvarez regards his father as a good influence on him. Santos frequently visits his boxing training camp to support him in his career. The same can be said about her mother, who remains close to the boxer.

His siblings are: The older brother of Canelo, his inspirational role figure, is Rigoberto Álvarez Barragán. The eldest of the Alvarez children, he was the first to pursue a boxing career. The winner of multiple titles, including the Mexican National Middleweight Champion, WBC Super Middleweight Champion, and many others, seems to be his brother Canelo's favorite boxer. Rigo and Canelo maintain good, warm relationships. For now, Rigo is retired In the field of boxing. Daniel is the second oldest brother of Saul Alvarez, a professional athlete. He was also a fighter, but he did not reach Saul's level. Another member of the boxing family is Ricardo, Saul's older brother. He, too, has accomplished several professional goals. In his career, Ricardo fought in 30 combat and won 24 of them. The former pro fighter Gonzalo Alvarez. His job, which began in 2008 and stopped after a year, was relatively brief. He's staying in Guadalajara now, in Jalisco, Mexico. He and his other siblings have a pleasant friendship with Canelo.

Another example of the agile breed is Juan Ramon Alvarez, dubbed Inocente by his supporters. He is also a successful athlete, and he holds multiple coveted awards, including the IBF Light Middleweight Champion. Ana Elda is Saul Alvares's only sister. Saul also sees a big heart for her. He shares pictures with his sister over media platforms occasionally. From their photos, this becomes clear that they are very close. Bryan is the stepbrother Saul from his father's side and a girl named Susana, whom he cohabited with the boxer's mother after the split. The police investigated Susana in 2012 regarding him. She blamed her ex for violence against women and refusal to compensate support money.

. . .

Álvarez learned horseback riding on the farm as a child. Initially, he did not have any plans to go into boxing. This changed when he got bullied about his fair complexion and red hair. He got called names like "Jícama con Chile," translated as turnip with chili flakes, a famous Mexican snack. His bullies backed off when he was getting quite good at boxing.

When he was only ten years old, the young Álvarez got his first boxing gloves from his eldest brother, Rigoberto. Rigo was Canelo's role model and inspiration for starting the sport. He was also the first Álvarez to venture into boxing. When Rigo made his professional debut, Canelo was hooked to the sport.

Álvarez made his way into the Julian Magdaleno Gymnasium, famous for the father-son duo training team, Jose "Chepo" and Eddy Reynoso. The duo had a reputation for grooming champions in the sport. Among them are featherweight boxers, Javier Jauregui and Oscar Larios. It was in this gym that the name Canelo Álvarez was born. Chepo would address Alvarez by this name, and unlike the bullying he used to receive from his features, this one had good intentions. Thus, Canelo Álvarez is born.

Shortly after the young Canelo turned fifteen, he was advised by Jose Reynoso to drop out of high school and consider becoming a professional boxer. Initially, two of his competitors were knocked out in a row. He struggled with Miguel Vasquez in 2008, beating him at the end of the fourth quarter. Two years later, he and Gabriel Martinez won that game. Just after the twelfth round, the latter one declined to continue fighting.

As a consequence, Canelo received a belt from WBA Fedecentro. When he was 20, he became the World Championship runner-up. He knocked out Luciano Leonel Cuello to have the title.

CHAPTER 5

CANELO ÁLVAREZ'S PERSONAL RELATIONSHIPS

THE DATING LIFE of Canelo Álvarez is very productive. He's been dating loads of stunning and famous women. The beauties of Kate del Castillo (an actress), Shannon de Lima, the ex-wife of singer Marc Antonio, who is Jennifer Lopez's ex-husband, are also on the romantic lists. In addition to that, he has four children with four different moms. Álvarez is popular among ladies. He has had a significant number of relationships throughout his boxing career. His first recorded romantic relationship was with his high school sweetheart Karen Beltrán. He was only 17 when they welcomed a baby girl, Emily Cinnamon Alvarez, in 2007. The couple separated soon after the baby's birth. Álvarez and Beltrán never married, but he still takes responsibility for the child. He is often accompanied by a girl called "my little princess" at events and other significant activities.

. . .

In 2009, Álvarez, now 19 years old, was engaged to Marisol Gonzalez. The couple dated for nine months before getting engaged. Gonzalez was a former Miss Mexico Universe in 2003. She was eight years his senior. The wedding, scheduled for 2010, was canceled when the two decided to call it quits. Later, the boxer was caught getting cozy with actress Kate del Castillo, older than him by 18 years. They split up shortly in 2012. In 2013, he briefly dated Cynthia Rodriquez and "moved on" after months.

Later, it was known that Álvarez was in a secret relationship with Valeria Quiroz when he was dating Marisol Gonzales. Their relationship bore him a second daughter named Mia Ener Álvarez. Valeria keeps out of the spotlight because of his relationship with Mexican drug lord Joaquín "El Chapo" Guzmán. Mia is Canelo's second-oldest daughter. She is the consequence of his relationship with Valeria Quiroz, a model. The girl resides in Los Angeles with her.

Maria is the youngest daughter of Canelo. His children are primarily from different moms. Maria's mother's name is Fernanda Gómez. Through their mutual friend, who worked for yet another famous athlete, Oscar De La Hoya, she got to know the athlete.Álvarez first met Fernanda Gomez at a gala in October 2016, and they became a couple. They mostly keep the details of their relationship private, but it is known that they are an on-off couple. However, when Gomez announced she was pregnant with Álvarez's child, the boxer started another relationship with Shannon de Lima. The Venezuelan model just got divorced from singer-songwriter Marc Anthony. Alvarez's and de

Lima's fling was short-lived and only lasted for a couple of months before separating. De Lima went on record to say that although their relationship was quick, he sees Álvarez as a good person.

In September 2019, Álvarez welcomed another child, a baby boy, with business partner Nelda Sepulveda. Saul Adiel Álvarez is the fourth child of Canelo Álvarez. Álvarez and Sepulveda had a joint business venture in the ice cream business called Santos Sabores. Additionally, he was linked to Mexican singer-songwriter and actress Belinda Peregrin and beauty queen Barbara Turbay.

In February 2020, he appeared to be with Fernanda Gomez again and took to Instagram to post a photo of them on vacation. Gomez replied, "I love you." Today, the boxer remains a bachelor.

CHAPTER 6

THE RISE OF CANELO ÁLVAREZ

THE FIRST TIME Canelo Álvarez got in the ring was when he was 15 years old. He received medals at the Junior Mexican National Championships in 2004 and 2005, silver and gold, respectively. As an amateur, his record was 44-2 with 12 knockouts. Chepo Reynoso's encouragement left school and turned professional when he was 15 years old. In the first 1.5 years as a pro, he could knock out 11 of 13 boxers he faced. Álvarez proved to be a talented boxer as he won one match after the other. The Jalisco welterweight title was the first official title win. On August 31, 2007, the bout happened where he fought against fellow Mexican Ricardo Cano. Today, Álvarez holds the major titles WBC light middleweight, WBA (Unified) light middleweight, WBC middleweight twice, WBO light middleweight, WBA (Super) middleweight, IBF middleweight title, and WBO lightweight heavyweight title and the secondary title WBA (Regular) super middleweight.

. . .

Alvarez had not even fought a named opponent in the first 40 matches of his career to impress the Western citizen. While he was mentioned on the fight card of Floyd Mayweather Jr.'s Miguel Cotto fight, clashing with three-division world champion and future Hall of Famer Shane Mosley, he did get a chance. Through October 2018, with the sporting streaming platform DAZN, Alvarez agreed on a 5-year, 11-fight agreement worth roughly $365 million. The transaction at the moment was the highest in athletics. Alvarez's offer surpassed the terms of the six-fight, 30-month Showtime deal with Floyd Mayweather Jr., which had a $200 million commitment. At the same time, Mayweather gained additional funds from the PPV revenue created from Showtime. Alvarez progressed and, facing Cotto, has become a more efficient boxer. Canelo has won first place in several tournament matches over his career. Although there was one game in 2013 that he did lose. Then he met a more significant competitor in the ring – the iconic Floyd Mayweather. Alvarez's loss was predictable – Floyd was far more skilled at that moment and had begun his career nine years earlier than Canelo.

Alvarez showed progress defensively and offensively as he used his outstanding counterpunching to drive him to a majority decision victory and the WBC middleweight championship. The match on PPV did better than anticipated, producing over 900,000 sales and $58 million at the period, becoming the first occurrence to make about 900,000 PPV purchases not headlined by Mayweather, Manny Pacquiao, Oscar De La Hoya. This match makes Alvarez one of the professional sport's biggest names, as it proved he could bear the weight and produce figures that a very few could only achieve. Questions followed Alvarez heading into Golovkin's clash. In September 2017, many thought Golovkin did well enough to secure their initial match. Since earning a six-month sanction for a set of failed drug tests in February 2018, Alvarez's credibility was still on track, which delayed the subsequent clash from May to September. Alvarez managed three out of the four big middleweight world titles at middleweight. But Alvarez insisted on making other records by going up to two weight classes to fight WBO light heavyweight champion Sergey Kovalev rather than seeking to be the next unquestioned 160-pound champion. Kovalev had gained notoriety over the 175-pound division for most of the decade, but his best days are now behind him. While using the jab to precision and getting Alvarez on the ropes, Kovalev showed better performance than anticipated. Inevitably, however, when he knocked out Kovalev of becoming a four-division world champion, Alvarez's strength proved it might have an impact 15 pounds beyond his normal fighting weight.

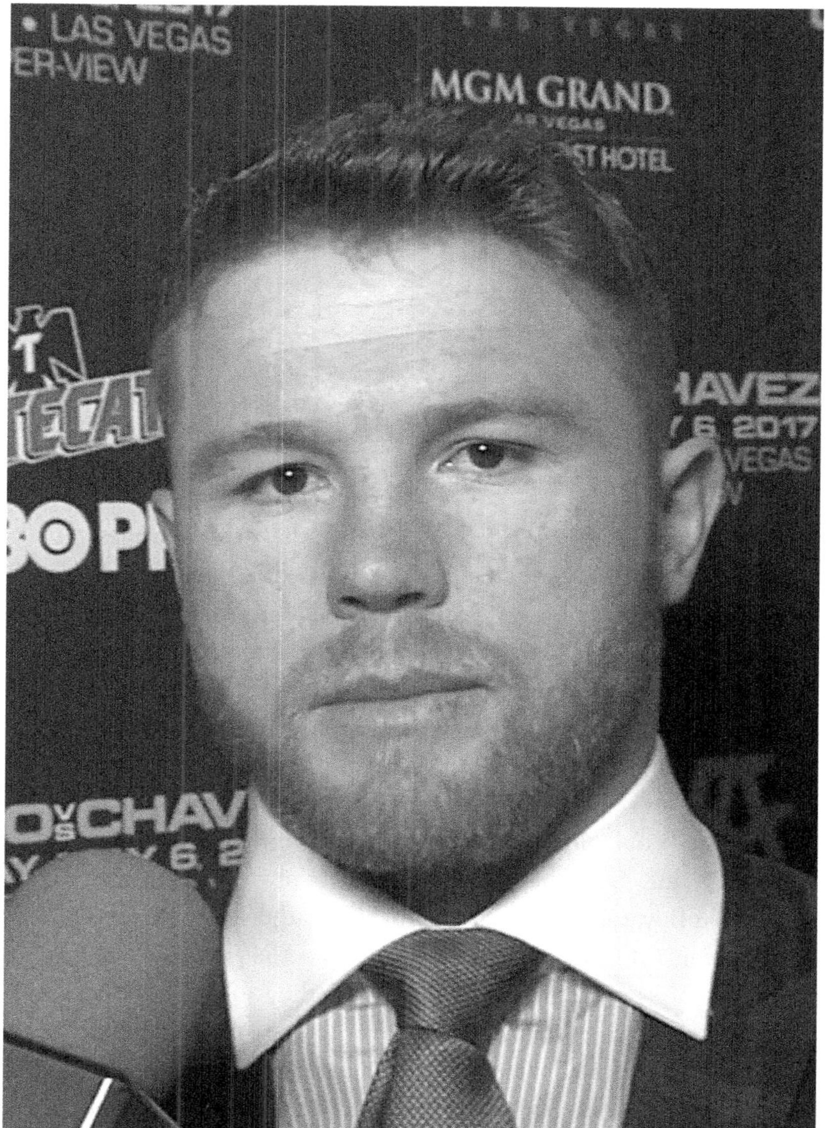
• LAS VEGAS
ER-VIEW
MGM GRAND
ST HOTEL
HAVEZ
6 2017
VEGAS

CHAPTER 7

CANELO ALVAREZ IS PROBABLY the world's biggest boxing superstar. Since he was 15 years old, Alvarez, 29, has already been boxing extensively. In four weight divisions, namely his most recent match, he captured several world titles when he moved up two weight classes in November and knocked over Sergey Kovalev to take the WBO light heavyweight championship in the 11th round. One cannot deny the skill and machismo Álvarez shows in the ring. People flock to arenas to catch a glimpse of boxing's newest star. Soon he got the attention of Top Rank and Golden Boy, top promotion companies in the sport. Richard Schaefer, CEO of Golden Boy, recalled that Álvarez was very famous at such an early age, and they jumped at the opportunity to work with him once he was old enough to fight in the United States. "With a majority decision over Gennady "GGG" Golovkin on September 15 in Las Vegas, Alvarez won the WBA, WBC, and lineal middleweight championships. A year ago, it reminded their first encounter that resulted in a split tie. Just after the rematch, Alvarez had become a network-free agent and eventually had become the highest-paid player in sports by accepting a five-year, $365 million deal to compete strictly on DAZN.

To date, Canelo Álvarez holds The Ring magazine titles middleweight and light middleweight, the lineal title middleweight twice, regional titles Jalisco welterweight, WBA Fedecentro welterweight, WBC-NABF welterweight, WBO Latino welterweight, WBC Youth welterweight, WBC Silver light middleweight, and honorary titles WBC Diamond middleweight title, WBC Franchise middleweight title.

Among the numerous awards he won are the 2012 Premio Juventud for Promising New Player in Sports, the 2019 Hispanic Heritage Award in Sports, the 2019 Best Boxer ESPY Award, 2019 The Ring magazine's Fighter of the Year, and 2020 Premio Juventud for Influencer With A Cause.

CHAPTER 8

CANELO ÁLVAREZ'S FRIENDS AND FOE

THE ONLY LOSS in Álvarez's professional record was handed to him by American boxer Floyd Mayweather Jr. The match happened in the MGM Arena in Las Vegas on September 14, 2013. Throughout the fight, Álvarez maintained his composure, but the more experienced Mayweather bested him. The result was in favor of Mayweather by decision.

Álvarez developed a friendship with Kazakhstani professional boxer Gennadiy Golovkin also known as GGG. Before parting ways, the two used to go to the same training camps for around two years. Si Boxing reported that they "spar together, lift weights together, eat and run and take breaks together... extending beyond the confines of any boxing ring and into nights out together in California." Golovkin also admitted that it was Álvarez who got him into Mexican music.

. . .

A few years later, they faced each other for the unified WBA (Super), WBC, IBF, IBO, Ring magazine, and lineal middleweight championship. The result was a controversial draw, which led to a rematch, September 15, 2018. Álvarez claimed success in this match named The Ring magazine as the "Fight of the Year 2018. A third fight was scheduled in September 2020, but due to the COVID-19 crisis, it was moved to May 2021.

CHAPTER 9

FUN FACTS ABOUT CANELO ÁLVAREZ

EVEN AFTER ALL HIS success in boxing, Álvarez still likes to go horseback riding, a hobby he developed when he was young and living on their family farm. Today, this is a hobby he pursues on the weekend or as a way to wind down from boxing. He has been the youngest of seven siblings. Both of them are now expert boxers. His family takes pleasure in their boxing ability. As far as boxing goes, Canelo is the most prominent among his fans. At 15 years of age, he rose to fame. He had no thoughts about becoming an experienced boxer.

He dropped out of secondary school in 2005 by becoming a pro fighter. He had just reached 15 then. Before he got 18, he played 34 matches.

· · ·

Canelo supposed to mean is "cinnamon" in Spanish. Canelo is not the forename of Alvarez. It's Saul. Since he has red hair, Canelo is his alias. His trainer names him canelito or little cinnamon due to his freckles and red hair. It makes him look like he's got cinnamon poured on him. The "little" was removed as he matured.

CHAPTER 10

HOW THE WORLD SEES CANELO ÁLVAREZ

CANELO ÁLVAREZ HAS COME a long way since he started as a 15-year old boxer. His is a rag to riches story, filled with hard work, determination, and talent. Today, everyone in the boxing world knows his name. In 2019, he was hailed as Forbes' Top 4 World's Highest-Paid Athletes. He earned a total of $94 million, $2 million of which are only from brand endorsements. DAZN by Perform Group-owned premium online streaming business roped in Canelo Alvarez among its key influencers in 2018. The five-year, 11-fight deal was determined to be equivalent to $365 million. Roger Dubuis, the watchmaker, pledged to accept Canelo Alvarez in 2018. Canelo owns and promotes the products and carries the company's logo on his pants in crucial matches as Roger Dubuis' brand ambassador. Early in 2016, Canelo Alvarez teamed up with Tecate and Hennessy, the finest Cognac in the globe, in 2018, opted to be among Canelo's associates. Coppel was a departmental shopping mall located in Mexico, which Canelo supported.

In 2019, to help him handle his vast wealth, Canelo collaborated with a financial services agency, Value Grupo Financiero.

Little is known about the boxer's personal beliefs, but some cite him as a Christian by religion. Canelo isn't religious, and in prose, he has yet to offer information regarding his convictions. Moreover, as a non-believer, he has not made announcements or actions that provide him back. Therefore, his place of faith matters resides anywhere within the eyes of the public.

Álvarez is big on philanthropy as he was reported to help out earlier in his career. In 2011, he partnered with the Youth Institute to build a youth house. He held motivational youth talks in numerous regions in Veracruz. In 2017, he donated $1 million to relief efforts like medicine, supplies, food, and construction materials after September's 7.1 magnitude earthquake hit central and southern Mexico. In 2020, he donated 500 000 pesos to Nariz Roja AC, giving aid to cancer children. In that same year, he joined the fight with COVID-19 as he donated 950 personal protection kits benefitting health workers on the frontline.

Today, Canelo Álvarez stands as a testament that anyone can achieve anything if they put their mind to it. Only in his 30's, he shows no sign of stopping as he continues to box his way to greatness. Canelo Alvarez is probably the world's biggest boxing superstar.

CHAPTER 11

REFERENCES:

HTTPS://WWW.SPORTINGNEWS.COM/US/ BOXING/NEWS/WHAT-ITS-LIKE-FIGHTING-CANELO/EMOJEURTFXHQ1IW8BK22XOF70

https://www.latimes.com/sports/boxing/la-sp-canelo-alvarez-daniel-jacobs-peaking-20190502-story.html

https://www.boxingnewsandviews.com/2017/08/12/canelo-irish/

https://ethnicelebs.com/canelo-alvarez

https://gossipgist.com/canelo-alvarez

https://fansided.com/2017/09/06/20-facts-canelo-alvarez/4/

https://familytron.com/canelo-alvarez/

https://www.unionjalisco.mx/articulo/2020/06/02/viral/las-ex-de-narcos-del-clan-chapo-que-fueron-amantes-de-boxeadores

https://www.latintimes.com/canelo-alvarez-relationship-rumors-fighter-may-have-2-year-old-daughter-169428

https://www.caras.com.mx/el-espia/nelda-sepulveda-bebe-del-canelo-alvarez/

http://www.playerwives.com/boxing/canelo-alvarez-girlfriend-shannon-de-lima/

https://www.essentiallysports.com/boxing-news-canelo-alvarez-the-playboy-heres-a-list-of-the-girls-he-has-dated/#:~:text=Saul%20Canelo%20Alvarez%3A%20Relationships&text=The%2019%2Dyear%2Dold%20Mexican,%2Dyear%2Dold%20Marisol%20Gonzalez.&text=5%20weeks%20after%20the%20engagement,their%20vows%20a%20year%20later.

https://www.sportswallah.com/boxing/relationships/boxer-canelo-alvarez-and-his-relationship-saga-over-the-years/

https://en.wikipedia.org/wiki/Canelo_%C3%81lvarez#Personal_life

https://www.google.com/search?sa=X&sxsrf=ALeKk02aQRpFiVTo9aYq5R-4F2M3EyS2OA:1603865761339&q=Premio+Juventud+for+Influencer+With+A+Cause&stick=H4sIAAAAAAAAONgFuLSz9U3MDOtMisvUOLVT9c3NMwwT7Esyq5KopLNTrbSTyxPLEqBkPHlmXl5qUVWYE7xI8YYboGXP-4JSwVPWnPyGqMvF371QhpcbK55JZkllUJyXHxSSPZqMEjxcCHxrZgomHgWsWoHFKXmZuYreJWWpeaVlKYopOUXKXjmpeWUpuYlpxYphGeWZCg4KjgnlhanAgB9pjMEyQAAAA&ved=2ahUKEwj5-eLHodbsAhXyKKYKHa3FDqMQri4wE3oECBgQMw

https://www.ringtv.com/587542-canelo-alvarez-named-ring-magazine-fighter-of-the-year-2019-all-category-winners-revealed/

https://en.wikipedia.org/wiki/Floyd_Mayweather_Jr._vs._Canelo_%C3%81lvarez

https://bleacherreport.com/articles/1774222-floyd-mayweather-vs-canelo-alvarez-results-round-by-round-analysis-and-recap

https://www.dazn.com/en-US/news/boxing/canelo-ggg-3-2021-negotiations/7a2ycsze1tj911rqlw18dts3l

https://www.si.com/boxing/2017/06/27/gennady-golovkin-canelo-alvarez

https://www.boxingscene.com/photos-saul-alvarez-honored-veracruz-charity-work--37287

https://www.espn.com/boxing/story/_/id/20781190/canelo-alvarez-donates-1-million-mexico-earthquake-relief-efforts

https://www.publimetro.com.mx/mx/publisport/2020/02/13/canelo-alvarez-dona-medio-millon-pesos-ninos-cancer.html

https://www.boxingscene.com/canelo-alvarez-makes-big-donation-first-responders--148836

https://sportskhabri.com/2019/07/29/brands-that-have-allied-with-boxing-star-canelo-alvarez/

10 Interesting Facts to Know about Canelo Alvarez - Wildwood Harley

Canelo Alvarez record: Career fight results, stats, titles, highlights | DAZN News the US

10 Interesting Facts to Know about Canelo Alvarez - Wildwood Harley

Canelo Alvarez is closing out the wild year with Madison Square Garden debut (nypost.com)

CHAPTER 12

pill.com › people › canelo-alvarezpeoplepill.com › people › canelo-alvarezCached

On February 11, Shane Mosley was announced as Álvarez's next opponent on May for his WBC Light Middleweight title. Alvarez defeated Mosley after 12 rounds ...

https://www.famousbirthsdeaths.com/canelo-alvarez-bio-net-worth-facts/

Canelo Alvarez Net Worth (2020), Height, Age, Bio and Factswww.famousbirthsdeaths.com › canelo-alvarez-bio-net-worth-factswww.famousbirthsdeaths.com › canelo-alvarez-bio-net-worth-factsCached

Alvarez was born Santos Saul Alvarez Barragan on July 18, 1990, in Guadalajara, Mexico. His father, Santos Alvarez, was a farmer. He inherited his red hair ...

https://gossipgist.com/canelo-alvarez

Canelo Alvarez - Bio, Net Worth, Fight Time, Kovalev ...gossipgist.com › Biographygossipgist.com › BiographyCached

Nov 3, 2019 - Canelo Alvarez's bio and facts like Famous For, Early Life, Birthday, Parents, Siblings, Net Worth, Engaged, Marisol Gonzalez, Children, ...

https://www.boxnation.com/boxing-news/7-random-facts-about-canelo-alvarez/

7 Random Facts About 'Canelo' Alvarez | Boxing Newswww.boxnation.com › boxing-news › 7-random-facts-about-canelo-a...www.boxnation.com › boxing-news › 7-random-facts-about-canelo-a...Cached

Nov 19, 2015 - Santos Saul Alvarez Barragan was born in Guadalajara, Mexico on 18th July 1990, the youngest of eight children. His parents were farmers ...

https://www.forbes.com/profile/canelo-alvarez/

Canelo Alvarez - Forbeswww.forbes.com › profile ›

canelo-alvarezwww.forbes.com › profile › canelo-alvarezCa-chedSimilar

Alvarez pocketed roughly $50 million combined for his first two fights on DAZN but should earn at least $35 million per fight in the future. Boxing fans are clamoring ...

https://www.espn.com/boxing/story/_/id/19292903/meet-saul-canelo-alvarez-ring

Meet Saul 'Canelo' Alvarez - outside the ring - ESPN.-comwww.espn.com › boxing › story › meet-saul-canelo-alva-rez-ringwww.espn.com › boxing › story › meet-saul-canelo-alvarez-ringCached

May 2, 2017 - He was born of a humble "tapatia" family of eight children, in which the older son, Rigoberto, decided to take up boxing, inspiring the rest of the ...

https://www.famousbirthsdeaths.com/canelo-alvarez-bio-net-worth-facts/

Canelo Alvarez Net Worth (2020), Height, Age, Bio and Factswww.famousbirthsdeaths.com › canelo-alvarez-bio-net-worth-factswww.famousbirthsdeaths.com › canelo-alvarez-bio-net-worth-facts

https://en.wikipedia.org/wiki/Canelo_%C3%81lvarez

Canelo Álvarez - Wikipediaen.wikipedia.org › wiki › Canelo_Álvarezen.wikipedia.org › wiki › Canelo_Álvarez

https://gossipgist.com/canelo-alvarez

Canelo Alvarez - Bio, Net Worth, Fight Time, Kovalev, BoxRecord ...gossipgist.com › canelo-alvarezgossipgist.com › canelo-alvarez

Printed in Great Britain
by Amazon